D1256989

CODE RED
MAY 20, 2013

Oklahoma's Devastating May 2013 Tornado

by Miriam Aronin

Consultant: Roger Edwards
Meteorologist
Storm Prediction Center
Norman, Oklahoma

BEARPORT PUBLISHING

New York, New York

Credits

Cover and Title page, © AP Photo/Sue Ogrocki; 3, © Tulsa World; 4, © AFP PHOTO/VINCENT DELIGNY; 5, © AP Photo/The Advocate Messenger, Clay Jackson; 6, © Kyodo via AP Images; 6T, © Rhonda Crosswhite; 7T, © Malenda Grace Hader; 7B, © AP Photo/Steve Gooch; 8, © Todd Shoemake/Shutterstock, Inc.; 9, © AP Photo/Tony Gutierrez; 10, © AFP/Getty images; 11, © Andrea Booher/FEMA; 12, © iStockphoto.com/petrmasek; 13, © XNR Productions; 14–15, © Minerva Studio/Shutterstock, Inc.; 17R, © Andrea Booher/FEMA; 17L, © JAMES GIBBARD/Tulsa World; 18, © Gene Blevins/Reuters/Corbis; 19, © REUTERS/Richard Rowe; 20, © ZUMA Press, Inc./Alamy; 21, © AP Photo/Sue Ogrocki; 22, © ED ZURGA/EPA/Newscom; 23T, © CBS NEWS; 23B, © Thorpe / Splash News/Newscom; 24, © ZUMA Press, Inc./Alamy; 25, © Andrea Booher/FEMA; 26, © AP Photo/Mark Lucas; 27, © FEMA/Alamy; 28T, © Rhonda Crosswhite; 28B, © JAMES GIBBARD/Tulsa World; 29T, © Thorpe/Splash News/Newscom; 29C, © Action Sports Photography; 29B, © solarseven/Shutterstock, Inc.; 30, © Tulsa World; 31, © Tulsa World.

Publisher: Kenn Goin
Senior Editor: Joyce Tavolacci
Creative Director: Spencer Brinker
Photo Researcher: Editorial Directions, Inc.

Library of Congress Cataloging-in-Publication Data

Aronin, Miriam, author.
  Oklahoma's devastating May 2013 tornado / by Miriam Aronin.
      pages cm. — (Code red)
  Audience: Ages 7–12.
  Includes bibliographical references and index.
  ISBN-13: 978-1-62724-131-1 (library binding)
  ISBN-10: 1-62724-131-0 (library binding)
  1. Tornadoes—Oklahoma—Moore—Juvenile literature. 2. Moore (Okla.)—History—21st century—Juvenile literature. I. Title. II. Series: Code red.
  QC955.2.A766 2014
  363.34'9209766'38—dc23

2013036886

For more information, write to Bearport Publishing Company, Inc., 45 West 21st Street, Suite 3B, New York, New York 10010. Printed in the United States of America.

10 9 8 7 6 5 4 3 2 1

Contents

A Deadly Warning 4

From Teacher to Hero 6

Towering Twisters 8

Monster Tornadoes.................... 10

Tornado Alley............................. 12

Birth of a Storm 14

Out of Time! 16

"A Total Mess".......................... 18

Pulling People Out..................... 20

Lost Dog 22

Many Helpers............................. 24

A Safer Future............................ 26

Profiles 28

Glossary.....................................30

Bibliography 31

Read More..................................31

Learn More Online.....................31

Index..32

About the Author 32

A Deadly Warning

May 20, 2013, began as a normal school day at Plaza Towers Elementary School in Moore, Oklahoma. Just before 3:00 p.m., fourth-grader Damian Britton was in math class when he heard a loud siren. Damian knew what that sound meant—a **tornado** was coming! He and his classmates raced to find shelter.

The monster tornado approaching Moore

The students took cover in a nearby bathroom. Six of them huddled together inside one tiny stall. "Then we heard the tornado," said Damian. "It sounded like a train coming!" Luckily, the students were not alone. Sixth-grade teacher Rhonda Crosswhite had also taken shelter in the bathroom.

Some schools hold tornado **drills**. During drills, students practice finding safe places to hide in case a tornado strikes.

66 We heard the sirens go off and then we all ran into the hallway. **99**

–Damian Britton

From Teacher to Hero

As Ms. Crosswhite and the students huddled in the bathroom, the tornado **violently** shook the school. Powerful, swirling winds tore the roof off the building. Some of the walls crumbled to pieces or collapsed. The monster storm was ripping the school to shreds. Ms. Crosswhite threw her body on top of Damian and the other children. "We're going to be fine," she told them. "I'm protecting you."

Ms. Crosswhite

A damaged classroom at Plaza Towers Elementary School

Debris rained down on Ms. Crosswhite. "It felt like someone was beating me up," she said. Luckily, in a few minutes, the tornado passed. Ms. Crosswhite had painful cuts on her back and feet, but she and the children were safe. "She saved our lives!" said Damian.

Plaza Towers Elementary School before the storm

The remains of Plaza Towers Elementary School

The tornado's winds reached more than 200 miles per hour (322 kph). Winds that strong can blow a house down or toss a car more than 328 feet (100 m).

Towering Twisters

How do tornadoes like the one that hit Damian's school cause so much damage? A tornado is a fast-moving tube of whirling winds. As it spins over land, a twister can topple trees and destroy buildings. The extreme force of the wind makes tornadoes one of the most devastating kinds of storms.

A twister gets its dark gray color from the dust and dirt that its winds pick up from the ground.

Scientists rate tornadoes based on the damage they cause as well as their wind speed. Tornadoes are rated from 0 to 5 on the Enhanced Fujita (EF) scale. The one that hit Moore was an EF5—the strongest type of tornado.

Most tornadoes last only about ten minutes. However, the Moore tornado lasted for more than half an hour! As a result, the tornado destroyed a huge area 17 miles (27 km) long. It caused massive destruction in the cities of Moore, Newcastle, and southern Oklahoma City. When the tornado ended, large parts of Moore, including Plaza Towers Elementary School, had been turned into **rubble**.

Hundreds of houses flattened by the tornado in Moore

9

Monster Tornadoes

Amazingly, May 20, 2013, was not the first time a monster tornado hit Moore. The people of Moore have faced terrifying storms before. On May 3, 1999, a huge twister smashed into the city. Its fierce winds reached 302 miles per hour (486 kph). That's the highest tornado wind speed ever measured!

High winds carry debris through the air during a tornado.

A less serious tornado hit Moore on May 8, 2003. Luckily, no one died in that storm, but it did cause more than 400 million dollars in damage.

Heather Moore lived through both the 1999 and the 2013 tornadoes. "It was very, very similar," she said. "Cars were turned over. Some houses were half gone, some houses were all gone." Oklahomans were shocked that one city could be hit so hard twice.

The 1999 tornado lasted for about an hour and a half. Sadly, 36 people died as a result of that storm. It destroyed this and many other houses in Moore.

Tornado Alley

Why has Moore, Oklahoma, been hit by so many twisters? All tornadoes start from violent thunderstorms, which can happen anywhere in the United States. However, Oklahoma is located in an area where these powerful storms are most likely to form. This long stretch of land is called Tornado Alley.

Tornadoes start from violent thunderstorms, such as this one.

Tornado Alley is part of a large, flat area called the **Great Plains**. There, warm, moist air from the Gulf of Mexico mixes with cool, dry air from Canada. When strong winds and warm and cold air overlap, powerful thunderstorms form that can cause tornadoes. That is exactly what happened on May 20, 2013, in Oklahoma.

This map shows the location of Tornado Alley, the area in the United States where most tornadoes form.

Most of the world's tornadoes occur in the United States. Usually, about 1,000 twisters hit there every year.

Birth of a Storm

On May 20, 2013, **meteorologists** began tracking a growing storm near Moore. Their **radar** showed that the storm was rapidly developing dangerous high-speed winds. The storm's winds were also moving in different directions. When the winds passed over each other, they formed a swirling tube of air in the sky.

The Moore tornado developed from a huge, swirling thunderstorm like this one.

The whirling tube began to pull air up from the ground into the clouds. This was the start of the tornado. At 2:56 p.m., the storm appeared near Newcastle, Oklahoma. Then it headed toward Moore. The twister's wild winds lifted and shredded everything in their path. As the deadly tornado approached Moore, sirens sounded across the city.

Although all tornadoes start from thunderstorms, most thunderstorms do not cause tornadoes.

Out of Time!

The sirens were not the only warning Moore **residents** received. Gary England, a local meteorologist, also alerted TV viewers to the deadly storm. "If you are not underground, you will not survive this storm," he said. "You have run out of time."

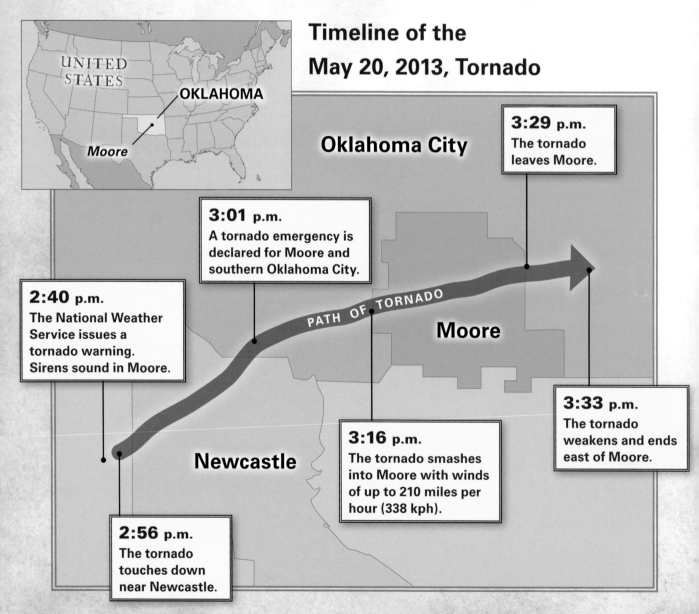

Timeline of the May 20, 2013, Tornado

UNITED STATES

OKLAHOMA

Moore

3:29 p.m.
The tornado leaves Moore.

Oklahoma City

3:01 p.m.
A tornado emergency is declared for Moore and southern Oklahoma City.

2:40 p.m.
The National Weather Service issues a tornado warning. Sirens sound in Moore.

PATH OF TORNADO

Moore

3:33 p.m.
The tornado weakens and ends east of Moore.

Newcastle

3:16 p.m.
The tornado smashes into Moore with winds of up to 210 miles per hour (338 kph).

2:56 p.m.
The tornado touches down near Newcastle.

Luckily, Moore residents Alfredo Corrales and Viviana Luna had a **storm cellar**. They crawled inside before the storm hit. Several neighbors crowded inside, too. Minutes later, the tornado struck. Alfredo heard a large tree snap in two and crash to the ground. As the wind roared, he pulled hard on the cellar door to keep it closed. If he let go, he was sure the door would be torn off into the huge twister.

One of the safest places to be during a tornado is underground in a storm cellar, out of reach of the powerful winds and flying debris.

66All the pressure from the wind speeds was just pulling up on the door.99

—Alfredo Corrales

"A Total Mess"

After the winds died down and the storm ended, Alfredo and Viviana left their shelter. They were shocked. Their whole neighborhood was in ruins. Viviana said, "It's just a total mess." Alfredo and Viviana were not the only ones affected by the tornado. Almost 4,000 homes and businesses in Moore were badly damaged.

> **"Trees were snapped in half. Roofs of houses were gone."**
>
> –Viviana Luna

The damaged buildings in Moore included this medical center.

One of the destroyed buildings was Plaza Towers Elementary School. When Damian Britton left the school after the storm, he couldn't believe his eyes. "It was just a **disaster**," Damian said. "There was just a bunch of stuff thrown around and the cars were tipped over."

The May 20 twister destroyed many cars near Plaza Towers Elementary School.

A total of 23 people died in the tornado, including seven students at Plaza Towers. About 240 more were injured.

Pulling People Out

After the storm, many people were trapped in the rubble from destroyed buildings. Alfredo had already saved his neighbors by sharing his shelter. Now he hurried to help more people. Alfredo kicked in a door to save a grandmother and her grandchildren. "The whole living room was just **obliterated**," he remembers.

Rescuers save people trapped at the Moore Medical Center.

Rescue workers raced to save more people injured or trapped by the storm. They searched for **survivors** in every ruined home. At Plaza Towers Elementary School, children and teachers were buried under the debris. Rescuers found them and carefully pulled them out. In the end, the rescue workers saved more than 100 people in Moore.

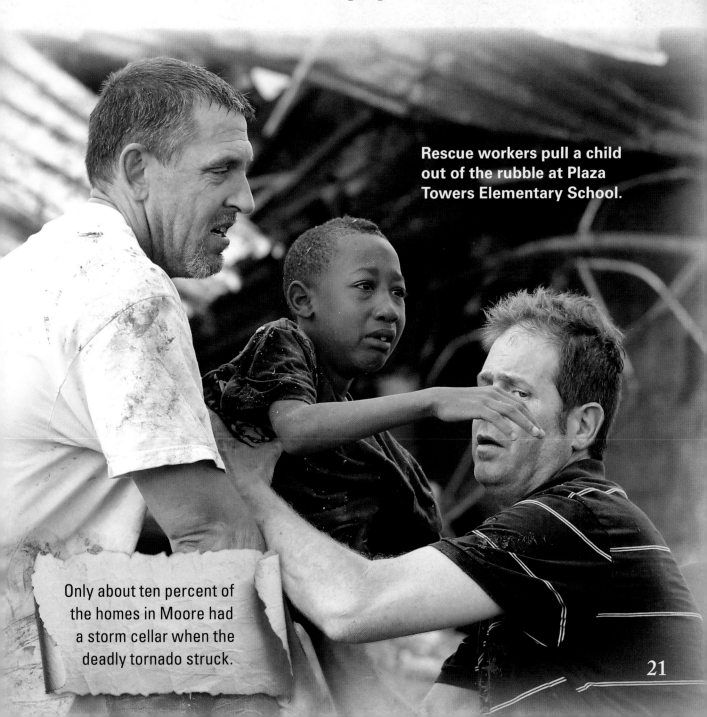

Rescue workers pull a child out of the rubble at Plaza Towers Elementary School.

Only about ten percent of the homes in Moore had a storm cellar when the deadly tornado struck.

Lost Dog

The storm not only harmed people, it was also very dangerous for animals. In all the confusion and destruction, many pets became separated from their owners. Without food and water, the animals could die.

Rachquel Brown's children were all in school at Plaza Towers when the twister hit. After the storm, they found each other quickly. However, the family dog, Charlie, was missing.

A shelter worker cuddles with a dog rescued from the storm.

Animal shelters worked hard to reunite owners with their lost pets. They even set up Web sites to help people find their animals.

The tornado had hit and destroyed the family's home while Charlie was still inside. The children had lost their school and their home. Had they lost their dog, too? Rachquel went to visit the ruined house after the storm. As she stared sadly at the rubble, she noticed something small and furry climb out. Rachquel gasped in shock. It was Charlie! Soon, the children and their pet were together again.

Rachquel finding Charlie in the rubble of her house

Rachquel Brown and her children after the storm

Many Helpers

Volunteers in Moore helped people find their lost pets. Many more people around the country also wanted to help. Some sent money, food, water, and clothing. Other volunteers came to the city to set up shelters for people whose homes were destroyed. They even helped Moore residents find medical care.

Many volunteers worked with the American Red Cross, a group that helps disaster survivors. It makes sure the survivors have food, water, shelter, medical care, and other basic needs.

The government helped, too. President Barack Obama sent workers from **FEMA** (Federal Emergency Management Agency) to Moore. FEMA **search-and-rescue teams** found and saved people hurt by the storm. Other FEMA workers helped people who had lost homes or businesses pay for repairs.

FEMA search-and-rescue workers in Moore

A Safer Future

After the storm, broken trees, pieces of crushed buildings, and ruined belongings covered the ground. Removing all of the debris would be a huge job. However, before the cleanup began, the city put up new street signs. Why? In neighborhoods that had been destroyed, the old street signs had blown away. The new signs helped rescuers and townspeople find their way through the city.

Volunteers help clean up a neighborhood in Moore.

What happened to the debris from the tornado? Old wood, paper, and clothing scraps were burned. Materials that could be used again, such as bricks, were saved.

After the cleanup, the huge effort to rebuild Moore began. The city wanted people to be safe from tornadoes in the future. Schools and homes were rebuilt to include storm shelters or cellars. Replacing all the damaged buildings would be hard work, but the townspeople knew they would have help along the way. "You face a long road ahead," President Obama told the people of Moore. "But you will not travel that path alone."

President Barack Obama visited Moore after the tornado to offer encouragement to residents.

Profiles

Many people showed great courage and compassion during and after the Moore tornado. Here are four of them.

Rhonda Crosswhite **was at Plaza Towers when the tornado hit.**

- Was a sixth-grade teacher at Plaza Towers
- Took cover in a school bathroom
- Threw her body over students, including Damian Britton, to protect them
- Had minor cuts from falling debris

Alfredo Corrales **was at home in Moore when the tornado hit.**

- Took cover with Viviana Luna in their storm cellar
- Saved his neighbors by sharing his shelter
- Helped rescue people who were trapped in ruined houses
- Kicked in a door to save a grandmother and her grandchildren

Rachquel Brown and her children lived in Moore when the tornado hit.

- Had three children who went to Plaza Towers Elementary
- Her home was destroyed in the tornado
- Was separated from the family dog, Charlie, during the storm
- Found Charlie in the rubble of her house

Barack Obama was president of the United States at the time of the tornado.

- Sent FEMA workers to Moore to help find and save people hurt by the storm, as well as to help people who had lost their homes and businesses
- Visited Moore to survey the damage caused by the storm
- Offered words of encouragement to the people of Moore

Glossary

debris (duh-BREE) scattered pieces of houses, buildings, or other objects left after a storm

disaster (duh-ZASS-tur) a terrible act of nature that happens suddenly and causes much damage

drills (DRILZ) exercises or activities that are practiced over and over

FEMA (FEE-muh) letters standing for Federal Emergency Management Agency; a U.S. government organization that helps communities prepare for and recover from natural disasters

Great Plains (GRAYT PLAYNZ) the grasslands of North America that cover much of the central United States and parts of Canada

meteorologists (*mee*-tee-ur-OL-oh-jists) scientists who study and predict the weather

obliterated (uh-BLIT-uh-*rayt*-uhd) completely destroyed

radar (RAY-dar) a tool that can find the location of an object by sending out radio waves that hit the object and bounce back to form an image on a computer screen

residents (REZ-uh-duhnts) people who live in a particular place

rubble (RUHB-uhl) broken pieces of rock, brick, concrete, and other building materials

search-and-rescue teams (SURCH AND RES-kyoo TEEMS) groups of people who look for survivors after a disaster, such as a tornado

storm cellar (STORM SEL-ur) a room below ground level used as a safe place to stay during storms

survivors (sur-VYE-vurz) people who live through a disaster or other horrible event

tornado (tor-NAY-doh) a rotating column of air that moves over land and can cause much destruction

violently (VYE-uh-*luhnt*-lee) acting with great force or strength

volunteers (*vol*-uhn-TIHRZ) people who offer to do a job without pay

A woman carrie
homa City suburb

BY RANDY ELLIS
The Oklahoman

MOORE — A
nado roared thr
and south Okl
on Monday, kil
51 people and le
workers frantic
ing for survivors
astated Plaza
mentary School
school district.
The state Me
iner's Office re
at least 51 peop
and said the
expected to rise
children were r
among the conf
talities.
Relatives wer
for children at P
saying more th
missing and f
as emergency
continued to wo
evening in hope
survivors. Relat
missi   ldren
grade

30

Plaza Towers was one
of two Moore elementary
schools ravaged by the massive tornado as it ground up

the debris. Emergency workers arrived quickly and began freeing the children.

Monday and was
on the ground
until 3:36 p.m.

Newcastle

Tornado's path covers
approximately 20 miles

SOURCE: National Weather Service

STEVEN RECKINGER/Tulsa World

school building that had
become a twisted heap of
bricks, blocks and iron.
The smell of gas was thick
in the air.

"They still aren't quite
sure on the number of who
might be missing," Fallin

SEE MOORE A5

SEE SCHOOL A4

Bibliography

Brown, Eryn. "Weather Conditions Were Ideal for the Tornado That Slammed Oklahoma." *Los Angeles Times* (May 21, 2013).

Fernandez, Manny, and Jack Healy. "Drama as Alarm Sirens Wailed: Time Reveals Lower Death Toll from Oklahoma City Tornado." *New York Times* (May 21, 2013).

Kim, Eun Kyung. "'Good Job, Teach': Educators Emerge as Heroes in Okla. Tragedy." *Today News* (May 21, 2013).

Perry, Bryan. "How Big Was the Moore, Oklahoma Tornado?" CNN (May 27, 2013).

Read More

Person, Stephen. *Saving Animals After Tornadoes (Rescuing Animals from Disasters).* New York: Bearport (2012).

Rudolph, Jessica. *Erased by a Tornado! (Disaster Survivors).* New York: Bearport (2010).

Simon, Seymour. *Tornadoes.* New York: HarperCollins (2001).

Learn More Online

To learn more about the May 2013 Oklahoma tornado, visit
www.bearportpublishing.com/CodeRed

ugh the Okla-

vors
school

oore tornado
A4
nday's weather,
nadoes. A6
gh School coach;
anything like

ue dogs arrived
niffing through
Then the sound
mers could be
he rubble.
overnor con-
children's bod-
n found at the
also confirmed
of adults had
on the school

ll aren't quite
number of who
missing," Fallin

SEE **SCHOOL** A4

Victims of Sunday's tornadoes assess devastation

Index

American Red Cross 24
animal shelters 22

Britton, Damian 4–5, 6–7, 19
Brown, Rachquel 22–23, 29

Charlie 22–23, 29
cleanup 26–27
Corrales, Alfredo 17, 18, 20, 28
Crosswhite, Rhonda 5, 6–7, 28

debris 7, 21, 26–27, 28

England, Gary 16
Enhanced Fujita (EF) scale 8

FEMA 25

Great Plains 13

Luna, Viviana 17, 18, 29

meteorologists 14, 16
Moore, Heather 11
Moore, Oklahoma 4, 9, 10–11, 12,
    14–15, 16–17, 18–19, 21, 24–25,
    26–27, 28–29

Newcastle, Oklahoma 9, 15, 16

Obama, President Barack 25, 27, 29
Oklahoma City, Oklahoma 9, 16

pets 22–23, 24
Plaza Towers Elementary School
    4, 6–7, 9, 19, 21, 22, 28–29

radar 14
rescuers 20–21, 26
rubble 9, 20, 22–23, 29

storm cellars 17, 18, 21
street signs 26
survivors 21, 24

thunderstorms 12–13, 14–15
Tornado Alley 12–13
tornado drills 5

volunteers 24–25

winds 6–7, 8, 10, 13, 14–15,
    16–17, 18

About the Author

Miriam Aronin is a writer and editor in Chicago. She enjoys reading, dancing, knitting, and avoiding natural disasters.